WORLD WAR II

THROUGH
RUSSIAN
EYES

WORLD WAR II
THROUGH RUSSIAN EYES

PHOTOGRAPHS FROM THE RUSSIAN CENTRAL ARMED FORCES MUSEUM

Bartleby Press
Silver Spring, Maryland

Descriptions of photographs are from
Russian Central Armed Forces Museum records
and translated from the Russian by Robin Schwartzman and Igor Barsegian.

Published by:

Bartleby Press
11141 Georgia Avenue
Silver Spring, MD 20902

ISBN 0-910155-37-2

Printed in the United States of America

An Introduction

I spent hours pouring over thousands of neatly catalogue cards with attached vintage World War II photographs, thunderstruck by the beauty of the images, even among the most savage circumstances. Russian photographers who covered the World War II were among the very best in the world, rivaling American war photojournalists and photographers.

It was clear from the first moment the depth and breadth of the collection of photographs carefully stored at the Russian Central Armed Forces Museum and that a book should be published of some of the most noteworthy of these World War II images. It is an integral part of the exhibition being mounted and displayed throughout the United States beginning in Washington, D. C.

This book is dedicated to the Russian photographers and their subjects, people who suffered untold and unspeakable tragedies in a world war that crossed over their doorsteps into their lives and their homes. The only frustration is that more of the images could not be included in this small volume. Fortunately, in close cooperation with Colonel Alexander Nikonov and his dedicated and talented staff at the Russian Central Armed Forces Museum, more work will be done to give the world an opportunity to view more of their unique and historic holdings.

Full credit and gratitude is due to Kermit Weeks, President of the Historical Achievements Museum and Fantasy of Flight in Polk City, Florida. Mr. Weeks the primary reason access was gained to the Russian Central Armed Forces Museum in Moscow and for the partnership which has grown with Colonel Nikonov and his staff, which bodes well for many future creative endeavors. Special thanks are due to Colonel Alexander Nikonov. We also owe a great debt of gratitude to Mihail Yakovenko, Chief of the Depositories; Vladimir Lukin, Chief of the Research Group and Displays and Valentina Bogdanovich, Chief of the Photographic and Negative Archives.

Mr. Weeks enthusiasm, creahen realized has made this book, the entire exhibition, "World War II Through Russian Eyes," and the positive relationships in Moscow a reality. This will surely lead to many great accomplishments in the future. Douglas Marcille has tended to every detail with grace and endless energy making problems disappear. Viktor Kousnetzov prompted the entire enterprise one day with his reminiscence of meeting Mr. Weeks and soldering the vital connection with Colonel Nikonov, making all subsequent achievements history.

Absorb the emotional intensity, gravity, and sheer raw beauty imparted by fleeting, long ago shutter snaps of unknown Russian photographers. These images are momentary scenes from a tortuous war which scarred the hearts and souls and the very depths of an entire people. To this day, it colors their view of the world in ways much different from those whose borders were not pierced. The Russians, our allies in World War II, called it The Great Patriotic War. It still prompts reactions today as if the memories have been engraved upon their eyes—a screen through which every Russian judges events past, present and future. Now that the Cold War has ended and the wall between our peoples has literally fallen, understanding this history will enable us to assure that it is never be allowed to occur between us ever again. These images should help us better focus upon those long ago realities, punctuating the need to assure there will be no repetition for our children and theirs in the new millennium.

MARK ELLIOTT TALISMAN
EXHIBITION DIRECTOR AND AMERICAN CURATOR
WASHINGTON, D. C.
AUGUST 1998

Moscow, June 1941. Representative of the regional committee of the Communist Party for the Kievski region of Moscow, P. V. Paromonov (left) explains the tasks ahead to a group for defense of the revolutionary order.

Unknown, July 1941. *(top)* The Red Army on the front lines. Captured German soldiers and officers.

Unknown, July 1941. *(bottom)* The front-line army: Interrogation of a German prisoner.

Leningrad, July 1941. *(top)* Schoolchildren of the October region post placards on the street.

Moscow, August 1941. *(bottom)* On Gorki Street [downtown Moscow].

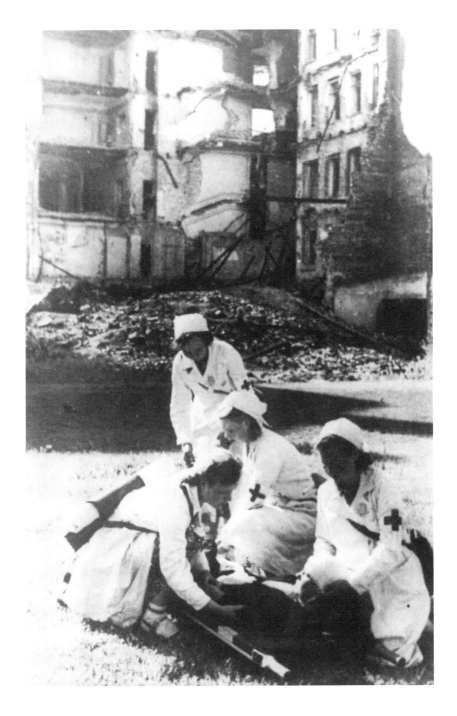

Unknown. Members of the medical brigade give first aid to a wounded person.

Leningrad, September 1941. A direct hit by an enemy shell on a residential building.

Neva River, October 1941. Preparation for a forced crossing of the Neva River in the Nevskaya Dubravka Region by the troops of the Eighth Army.

Moscow, November 1941. Barricades at the Kirov gate.

Moscow, November 1941. The cavalry passes through Red Square.

Unknown, November 1941. The front-line army on the Western front. Soldiers of the sub-unit of Lieutenant Kiril'tsev fire mortars at the enemy on the distant approach to Moscow.

Moscow, December 1941.

Moscow, 1941. The windows of TASS on Gorki Street.

Moscow, 1941. Graves of fascists on the far outskirts.

Leningrad. 1941. Evacuation of citizens of Leningrad.

Moscow, 1941. Women post placards on the streets.

Unknown, 1941. "On the icy road at night."

Moscow, 1941. Welding "hedgehog" barriers.

Stupino, Moscow District, 1941. Major General P. A. Belov, Commander of the First Guard Cavalry Corps, gives instructions to his commanders in the bomb shelter of an airplane factory.

Leningrad, April 1942. Fulfilling a military order at the Zhdanov factory: Packing mines.

Stalingrad, August 23, 1942. The antiaircraft guns defending the Stalingrad region repulse the air attack of the enemy.

Neva River, September 1942.

Stalingrad, October 1942. Antiaircraft gunners defending the industrial objects of the city.

Stalingrad, 1942-43.

Leningrad, 1942-43. "In the days of the blockade." Artillery shelling of Nevski District.

Lokotnya, date unknown. Nazi destruction in the village Lokotnya near Moscow. A young woman victim of a German raid is pulled from the wreckage of a house.

Stalingrad, 1942-43.

Stalingrad. October 1942. The command post of the 13th Guard Division.

Stalingrad, December 30, 1942. The people greet the shock unit commanded by Major Nikonov.

Unknown, December 1942. A soldier captures a German pilot from a downed Messerschmidt ME-109.

Stalingrad, December 1942. The front-line army in Stalingrad. "The German command hides from its soldiers the damage done to the fascist occupiers by the Red Army. In the units of the 'n' division agitators [infiltrators] have been appointed to inform the German soldiers about the successes of the Red Army."

Moscow, Winter 1942. Bodies of residents of a village near Moscow, killed by the Germans.

Moscow. 1942. Many enemy planes were downed above Moscow.

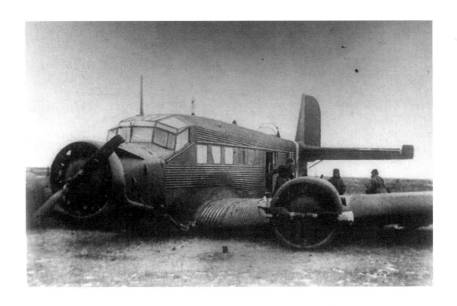

Stalingrad, December 1942. A German transport Junker Ju-52 airplane downed near Stalingrad.

Moscow, 1942. "Fighters defending the capital."

Stalingrad. 1942. A tank with the slogan "For the Motherland" battles in the ruins.

Moscow. 1942.

Stalingrad. 1942. A column of captured Germans.

Stalingrad. 1942. Commander of the Stalingrad Front General
Lieutenant A. I. Gremenko awards a medal to the defenders.

Orlov, Date unknown.

Unknown. Downed German plane.

Stalingrad, 1942-43. The Red Guards of the reconnaissance company of Lieutenant Levchenko reconnoitering the outskirts of the city.

Kukhtinka, 1942. The village of Kukhtinka after the retreat of the Germans.

Leningrad, 1942-43. Defense construction: Citizens of Leningrad build anti-tank fortifications.

Stalingrad, 1942. A battle in the factory shops at the "Barricades" factory.

Stalingrad, 1942. *(top)* At the front, soldiers of the regiment commanded by Colonel I. P. Levin fire mortars at the attacking fascists.

Leningrad, 1942-1943. *(bottom)* "Waiting for a signal."

Stalingrad. 1942. Construction of an assault bridge across the Volga.

Stalingrad, 1942. Command post of the headquarters of the 62nd Army on the bank of the Volga, opposite the "Barricades" factory.

Unknown, 1942-43. "The air pirates were hunting for them."

Leningrad, 1942-43. "In the days of the blockade. The first efforts at rebuilding."

Rzhava, date unknown. Railroad station near Rzhava. Senior Lieutenant Comrade Krenits reports on the course of military actions.

Leningrad, 1942-43. "Invitation to revenge." [The legend on the placard reads "Death to the Child Killers."]

Leningrad, 1942-43. "Citizens of Leningrad."

Leningrad, 1942-43. *(top)* A scene from the play "The Sea is Wide."

Leningrad. 1942-43. *(bottom)* The placard in the picture says "Long live the Motherland! Long live Stalin!"

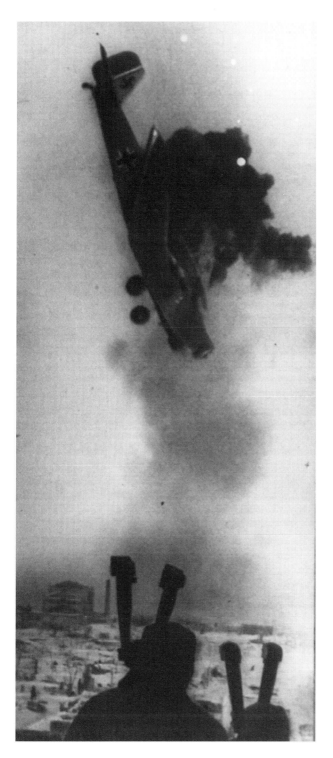

Stalingrad, January 1943. A Junker-52 transport plane downed by artillery fire.

Lake Ladoga, January 1943. Soldiers of the of the Red Army set out to comb the forest (south of Lake Ladoga). January 1943.

Leningrad, January 1943. *(top)* Breaking through the blockade. One of the sectors of German fortifications erected around Leningrad.

Salingrad, February 2, 1943 *(bottom)* The Soviet flag was raised over the ruins of the city on the Square of the Fallen Fighters. "The liquidation of the surrounded German-fascist troops in the Stalingrad Region was completed."

Unknown, January 1943. Captive German soldiers and officers, captured by a unit of the guard of General-Major Denisenko.

Unknown. Pouring ballast from a quarry into railroad cars.

Stalingrad, 1942-43. Street fighting.

Unknown. "They had two exits."

Stalingrad, February-March 1943 Road signs.

Stalingrad, February-March 1943. German cemetery in the village of Gorodishche.

Moscow, 1942. *(top)* Moscovites watch the premier of the ballet "The Humpbacked Horse."

Leningrad, 1942-43. *(bottom)* "Tickets are sold out."

Stalingrad, February-March 1943. After an air raid.

Voroshilovgrad, April 1943 A German airplane knocked out near
Voroshilovgrad [Lugansk].

Leningrad, 1942-43. Torpedo boat on the Neva River.

Yasnaya Polnaya, date unknown. "Soviet troops drove the German occupiers out of Yasnaya Polnaya, the birthplace of the great Russian writer L. N. Tolstoy."
In the picture: A school library destroyed by the Germans.

Orel, 1943. The Germans converted one of the beautiful houses on the central square of Orel into a brothel for soldiers.

Krasnodar, July 1943. "The trial of the German-fascist invaders and their accomplices for atrocities in Krasnodar and the Krasnodar region during the occupation. The sentence was carried out." In the picture: The bodies of the traitors on the gallows in the city square of Krasnodar.

Unknown. On the Ladoga Road, the port Kabona. Unloading provisions from freight cars.

Leningrad, 1942-43. Patrol on the Neva River.

Kharkov, December 1943. "The trial about the atrocities of the German-fascist invaders on the territory of Kharkov and the Kharkov District during the period of their temporary occupation."

Unknown. "Prisoners captured by the unit of Comrade Belov."

Leningrad, 1943. Breaking through the blockade of Leningrad. The troops of the Leningrad and Volkhov fronts meet.

Orel, 1943. *(top)* North of Orel, in the central Ulyanovo region: "Collective farmer S. M. Beliayev and his son Tolya at the site of their home, burned by the Germans."

Orel. 1943. *(bottom)* A railroad bridge across the Orlik River, destroyed by the retreating Germans.

74

Kalinin, 1943. "The scout and Kazakh Komsomol member, Senior Sergeant S. Baigabulov, was awarded the Order of the Red Star and Medal for Bravery for his daring raids and for the capture of Germans in battles for the city Veleekie Luki on the Kalinin front.

Unknown. Katyusha rockets.

Orlov, date unknown.
The result of the raid of our heavy bombers on the German positions.
Orlov axis.

Velikie Luki, 1943. "A fascist airplane burns." In the foreground is the body of the pilot.

Krasnodar, 1943. *(top)* In liberated Krasnodar. Units of the Red Army march through Krasnaya [Red] Street on the way to the front.

Orlovsk-Kursk crossroads, 1943. *(bottom)* "Ambush."

Kromy, date unknown. "After the German-fascist occupiers were driven out of the city of Kromy, Orlovskaya District, pits were discovered near Kromy in the village of Bazhovo that held the bodies of 'Soviet people.' Hitler's butchers threw old men, women, and children into the pits, having first gassed them."

Gatchina, date unknown. The red flag is raised over liberated Gatchina.

Volkhov. 1941-44. "Our infantry advanced through snow-covered swamps and woods."

Orel, 1943. In the region north of Orel. Captured German soldiers and officers.

Unknown. Bombs explode at the Vyborg Station.

Orel, 1942-43. A German cemetery. Western front north of Orel.

Unknown. "Enemy planes are in the air. At the battle alert signal, crews run to man their large-caliber anti-aircraft guns. Sergeant N. I. Slesarev is in front."

Moscow, 1944. *((top)* Captured German soldiers and officers are marched through the streets of Moscow.

Unknown. *(bottom)* The Second Cavalry Guard Division. After presentation of the guard flag.

Lublin, 1944. Pile of bones and skulls taken from pits outside the fence of the Lublin concentration camp at the time of excavations by a Polish-Soviet commission investigating the atrocities of the Germans.

Warsaw. "The German occupiers divided Warsaw into three zones Polish, German, and Jewish. The fascists kept all three parts separate from each other." A wall fencing in the Jewish sector.

Danzig. March 1945. "Soviet people liberated by our troops near Danzig."

Oranienburg, 1945. Prisoners in the concentration camp.

Unknown. "Behind the barbed wire of a concentration camp."

Moscow, 1945. Fireworks.

Unknown. New Year tree [traditionally used in Russia rather than Christmas trees] marking a German grave. "Substitute New Year gifts: To the dogs, Hanses and Fritzes."

Lublin, 1944.
Majdanek death camp: Human remains ready to be burned.

Lublin, 1944. Ovens at the concentration camp Majdanek.

Unknown. Children at the barbed wire of a concentration camp.

Orel. 1945. The building on which the first flag was flown when the
Red Army entered the city.

Berlin, 1945. On the bank of the Spree River. The picture was taken on the last day before the storming of the Reichstag.

Berlin, 1945. Soldiers after raising the banner of victory above the Reichstag. With the banner of victory. Moliton Kantariya (left) and Mikhail Egorov

Berlin 1945. Aerial view of the Reichstag.

Berlin. 1945. Soviet soldiers at the Brandenburg Gate.

Berlin, 1945. A group of soldiers and officers of the Third Shock Army, who distinguished themselves in the storming of the Reichstag and in raising the banner of victory.

Berlin, May 1945. Allied flags at the airport. The planes of the allies landed here for the conference at which the surrender of Germany was signed. May 1945.

Berlin. May 1945. General Eisenhower and General of the Army Sokolovski.

Berlin, 1945. Tempelhof Airport on the day of the surrender. Arrival of the English and American representatives.

Berlin, 1945. At the signing of the Declaration of Defeat of Germany and its capture by the governments of the four allied powers.
In the picture: The moment of signing of the Declaration: Field Marshal Bernard L. Montgomery signs.

Unknown. "Our cause is just!"

Moscow, 1945. Captured German soldiers and officers are marched through the streets.

Moscow, May 9, 1945.

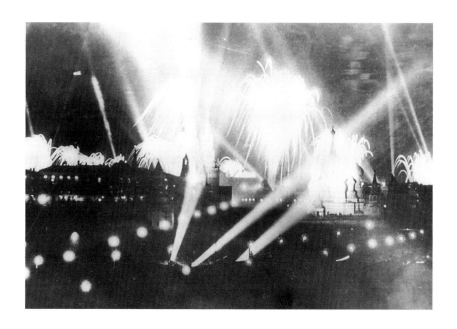

Moscow. May 9, 1945. Victory fireworks.

Moscow, May 9, 1945, 10:00 p.m. Victory Day, "To commemorate total victory over Germany, the capital of our Motherland, salutes the valiant troops of the Red Army and the Navy who scored this shining victory."

Moscow, May 1945. "The Holiday of Victory in Moscow alongside the Kremlin."

Bucharest, 1945. The people of Bucharest greet Soviets on Victory Day.

Moscow, 1945. "Victory Day." Fireworks.

Moscow, July 24, 1945. "The historic day of the Victory Parade,. The victorious soldiers brought these enemy flags which had been seized in battle to Red Square near the wall of the Kremlin and placed them near the granite base of Lenin's mausoleum."

Unknown, July 1945. German prisoners.

Moscow. 1945 Victory parade in Red Square, Marshal of the Soviet Union G. K. Zhukov passes the troops.